ANVIL, CLOCK & LAST

ANVIL, CLOCK & LAST

POEMS

Paulette Roeske

Louisiana State University Press   *Baton Rouge*
2001

Designer: Barbara Neely Bourgoyne
Typeface: Sabon
Printer and binder: Thomson-Shore, Inc.

Library of Congress Cataloging-in-Publication Data:
Roeske, Paulette.
   Anvil, clock & last : poems / Paulette Roeske.
   p. cm.
   ISBN 0-8071-2718-3 (cloth : alk. paper)—ISBN 0-8071-2719-1 (paper : alk. paper)
   I. Title: Anvil, clock, and last. II. Title.
   PS3568.O367 A84 2001
   811'.54—dc21
                                                                        2001000066

   The author gratefully acknowledges the editors of the following journals, in which some of the poems herein first appeared, sometimes in slightly different forms: *Ascent:* "Planting"; *Asian Studies in America:* "Chinese Acrobat, Age Six"; *Bluff City:* "My Father's Heart on Film"; *The Body Can Ascend No Higher* (chapbook): "A Matter of Interest"; *The Chariton Review:* "The Break of Day," "Guilt I," "Guilt II," "Half of the Story," "Summons,"; *Crab Orchard Review:* "So Long," "Mary Wilson-Formerly-of-The-Supremes" (as "Mary Wilson-Formerly-of-The-Supremes Sings Ooh-Baby Songs at The Nugget"; *The Georgia Review:* "Trust"; *The Journal:* "Too Much"; *Kaleidoscope Ink:* "Lesson," "Two Short Histories on a Single Theme (I)" (as "The Decivilizing of Harry Brown"); *The Threepenny Review:* "Anvil, Clock, and Last"; *Rhino:* "White Birch"; *Southern Indiana Review,* "Crinoline"; *Spoon River Poetry Review:* "Elephant Seals at Point Piedras Blancas," "Hibakusha," "Leaf and Wing."
   The following two poems are reprinted by permission: "Frozen Shoulder," which first appeared in *JAMA: The Journal of the American Medical Association* (September 27, 2000) vol. 284, no. 12: 1488, copyrighted 2000, American Medical Association; and "My Mother's Eye," which appeared in *JAMA: The Journal of the American Medical Association* (October 11, 2000) vol. 284, no. 14: 1754, copyrighted 2000, American Medical Association.
   "Trust" was reprinted in *Illinois Voices: An Anthology of Twentieth-Century Poetry from Illinois,* edited by Kevin Bradley and G. E. Murray, University of Illinois Press. "Too Much" was reprinted as a letterpress limited-edition broadside designed and hand-set by Pamela Barrie of Green Window Printers in conjunction with "A Formal Feeling Comes," a program hosted by The Poetry Center of Chicago. "My Father's Heart on Film" and "Planting" were reprinted in *The Body Can Ascend No Higher,* selected by Maura Stanton for the Illinois Writers Chapbook Award. "Hibakusha" was a finalist for the William Faulkner Poetry Award. "Anvil, Clock, and Last," "Lucky Death," and "After the Funeral" were finalists for the Phyllis Smart Young Prize, which is awarded for a group of three poems.
   The author wishes to thank The Mary Anderson Center for the Arts and the College of Lake County for support during the time some of these poems were written.
   These poems are for Lisel Mueller and John Van Doren, with gratitude for their wise and generous counsel; and for Robert Reid, who gave this book its happy ending.

This publication is supported in part by a grant from the National Endowment for the Arts.

NATIONAL ENDOWMENT FOR THE ARTS

The paper in this book meets the guidelines for permanence and durability of the Committee on Production Guidelines for Book Longevity of the Council on Library Resources. ∞

Goodbye
    At the visitation

Do not pity this body
insensible as stone,

two hands
weighted on its chest,

or grieve its slow dissolve,
beds of the veins—deserted.

Still, the halted tongue
cups its last syllable,

and the word I whispered
circles the cochlea's bony coil.

The still explosions on the rocks,
the lichens, grow
by spreading grey concentric shocks.
                    —Elizabeth Bishop

Love isn't a bomb bursting, though at the same time that's
    really what it is.
It's like an explosion that lasts a whole lifetime.
It comes out of that breakage they call knowing yourself,
    and then it opens wider and wider . . .
                    —Vicente Aleixandre

CONTENTS

I

Geode

Urging my fuchsia Schwinn named for a TV horse
up the steep hill behind my house,
I hunted rocks. Deep in the untillable fields,
I praised the stony ground, I kicked my shoes
to trash. Even the half buried
could not escape me.
I liked the big ones, drab as dirt or
sullen grey, the ochre of old bones. Like babies
I bundled them into a gunnysack,
cinched its neck with a length of rag,
and snapped it into the spring-loaded
book rack. I let out the reins, I sang
us all the way home.

In the alley behind the garage,
rapt in summer privacy
and blessed under the whinny and patient gaze
of my mare hitched to the fencepost,
I lined up my rocks in the wheel ruts.
Which would be first
to face my hammer's hard reality?
I remember the geode best, though
I'd never heard the word. Even now
I can conjure its solemn heft,
its dull phrenology. It got the same treatment
as the rest: a trip inside
to my garage-floor operating room,
a bath in the tin basin warming in the single square
of sun, a swaddle in the blanket I'd filched
from the linen closet, caution against blindness.
Hammer cocked in two hands behind my head,
every electric nerve alerted,
I held my breath.

Sometimes I missed or just grazed it,
skittered it out past a nest of rusty chains

where it ricocheted off the clanging
mower blades or sank into the silent wells
of old tires. I prayed
for the times the head struck true,
the rock cracked clean,
its perfect halves a seeded fruit
I saw in my turning mind *before*
I threw the blanket back. But
how could I have guessed the geode's
rare concentrics, its brilliant sharp-toothed crystals
deep within the dimpled mouth?
All summer I labored at my sweaty task.
It was hope that returned me to the hammer
to lay open the bright interiors
I could have overlooked.

Eye Test

When the big **E** on the chart
wavered just beyond clarity,
I was still learning to read.
Our teacher, Missouri Synod dour,
lined us up outside the cafeteria,
white sheet hung for privacy.
One by one we filed in, solemn
as novices. Instructed toward
the battered wooden desk,
which meant we'd learn a lesson, we watched
the screen flash **E**s in four positions:
the true one we knew from books
and its accomplice,
followed by a crippled stick dog
and an insect on its back.
We'd turn our young hands to prove
we could see.
When the traveling optician confirmed
even the biggest **E** was beyond me,
I grew smaller than I was.
The others saw shame
mimed in shadow on the sheet.
As for me, even now I put down my glasses,
indulging my hands in their old practice
of drawing the world up to my face.

Crinoline

Net, dipped in boiled Argo
then clipped with clothespins
to the line, that backyard artifact,
until it stiffened into shape to accentuate
the wasp waists of 50's girls
who hooped perfect circles of red felt
over layers of pale blue or pink
or snow white crinoline
starched to stand up by itself.
But when they sashayed
across the Dairy Queen parking lot
tonguing their soft-swirls into peaks,
cell by cell the net released its sequins
brightening their walk toward
the summer boys whose hearts
flared inside their chests,
sparked by the glittering ones,
bobby sox studded with rhinestone poodles,
mama and baby,
snapping at their ankles.

The Mangle

They kept the mangle in the basement.
The air was cool. Clothes lay in the basket.
Newfangled contraption, bigger than a stove,
it hissed and steamed. The rollers spun.
The mother sat in front of it, severe accountant,
calculating time in terms of clothes.
Her daughter was still young, longing
to be old enough to feed the fabric inch by inch
between its metal jaws. No match, no flint,
but still a fire devouring
fingers, hand, an arm pulled like a pillowcase,
machined down to the bone. The child shrank
from childhood—London Bridge and girls in a ring
whose whispers slipped between their fingers.

White Room

I am the wound and the knife!
—Charles Baudelaire

An ordinary office,
almost forgettable, in this case
a white oblong, unremarked by color.
Along one side, a white-sheeted table
where I lay, an ordinary child
brought for the medical routine
prescribed for girls my age.
Along the other, a row of straight-backed
chairs shoved against the wall. But for me
the view was up
into the relentless light from the fluorescent coil
that turned my white shirt blue,
shirt scrubbed, starched, and ironed
by my mother who sat in the second chair in her hat,
purse propped on her lap,
its amber handle a Roman arch,
her Sunday dress patterned with slanting rain
caught in dozens of tiny upturned umbrellas.
But I knew my shirt was really white,
clean. It stopped at my waist. Below,
the sharp bones of my hips—a cradle in which I lay,
my legs side by side, neatly socketed,
identical, as if posing a trick question that demands
Choose one.

When the doctor appeared,
he took my feet in his two hands
and pushed them toward me,
which meant my knees must bend.
Sliding his palms up my shins,
his fingers, those little climbers,
presented themselves on the horizon.
With one practiced gesture he pulled my knees apart,

ignoring the untried bones
that stuttered up two inches
for each inch he pushed down.

What did he see
in the frilled edges of the lips
he parted, flicked from side to side,
held, flicked again and kept on flicking
until he changed the rhythm with a finger
on the hood—what Klan or convent—he pulled back,
eyeing parts of me I had never seen
nor could put a name to. The knob
of his bald head shifting between my legs
forced my eyes to seek out my mother
who wouldn't look back.
In the first chair, my sister,
a solemn child of four
framed in ragged rabbit fur,
strings with pom-poms tied in a double goiter
beneath her chin,
girl pressed back against the slats
as if that could save her.

Around the light,
paint peeled back like skin
showed the plaster's rough texture,
an untidy map of craters
and dry rivers.

*

Sister, backed across the ocean
of that small room, you were my witness. Now,
far across the ribs of this uneasy continent
and on the edge of a real ocean,
you are home among the ardent bodies of your horses,
their breath enthralled by the early air,
steam rising from their haunches.
Locking the fingers of your bare hands,
you hold them out for my dirt-blackened boot,

a boost up,
the fingers of my left hand hooked
under the pommel, right leg
already swinging up and across the broad back
of this mare—agent of my future, shadow of my past.
                    In the paddock,
the others confer beside the electric fence.
Like children they watch us until we disappear,
the eucalyptus closing like a door behind us.
                    Heading down
into the shifting dunes, bracing against the skid,
she wrestles for the bit, bares her teeth
to tear at anything green then leaps the log
that would keep us off the beach, talks back
to the crop's hard syllables, tries to unseat me.
Suddenly mulish, she digs in her hooves
against me. I ride her badly, hard,
not out of malice or ignorance,
but because of who I am.

                    When I lead her home
lathered, in a temper, she shoves me up against
the gate. Reins wound around my fist,
she would drag me like a tail behind her.
Memory stumbles against rage.
I watch my left hand, gloved, lovely
in its stealth, fingers closing in four small taps
around the top rail, its attendant wire hot
to curb adventure. The long tongue
of the beach lolls below us. Plunging
her muzzle deep into the trough
she has always taken for granted, she does not know
I am the conduit through which the electric current
leaps to split open the day.
Head thrown back in silhouette
against the flawless sky,
the soft folds of her lips drawn back,
water coursing from the mouth shocked
open to show the metal bit,

eyes loose as change,
she does not scream
the way a horse can,
and in the silence pressed
against her open mouth
the other mares drift away,
bow out, count me out,
my sister said with her body,
her eyes caught on mine,
on me, the dark lamb,
out to the butcher whose bald head
crowned between my thighs
prized open in the white room,
silent except for the endless
sibilation of the fluorescent coil.

Two Short Histories on a Single Theme

I

At first it's the little things: drinking straight from
the faucet and eating asparagus with his fingers.
Then his wife notices he scratches his crotch in pub-
lic, at the shopping center, say, or at bridge parties.
He pees in the flowerbed if he thinks she isn't watch-
ing. That's when the neighbors start to talk. He
sleeps when he is tired—during sermons and at their
little Eva's wedding reception. Even when the band
plays "The Beer Barrel Polka," his favorite tune, and
the guests gallop past him, he's lost in a dream
where his life depends on undiscovering everything.
When he snores real loud, his wife jabs him in the
ribs. He jolts awake, ruffles his hair, then rubs the
crust from his eyes while trying to decide which of
the dancing girls he will take.

II

Listen, my sister says, our whole family is crazy. She
says I shouldn't need more proof than Uncle John, a
drunk who pulled the trigger five times before he
fell. But if I do, remember Mother with something
up her sleeve to spike the family stew or how
Grandmother Mary bit herself on the arm as a les-
son and left a mean scar shaped like a key. Or the
kids. Little Sally thinks her shoes are snakes and
Suzie beats her eyes black and blue. Bad genes, my
sister says, and don't even mention Grandfather Joe
going off the scaffold headfirst. Jesus that was no
accident. No one in the family talks about it except
my sister, and then only to me.

Lesson

Today, Schumann
and talk of where home is:
for "Träumerei," the key of F,
for Schumann, somewhere in Germany.
A small thought,
                but it sends me stumbling
through the rooms of my childhood
I've locked to dodge my mother's voice,
her white hands on everything,
rearranging whatever small order
I invented.

Over a hundred years ago in the asylum
Schumann turned from the angels
that dictated his secret themes,
then leapt from the bridge
into the Rhine.
                The teacher speaks
of Schumann-the-Romantic
and calls my study an adventure
even while admonishing me
to remember the signature,
the instruction to come back home
to the key that opens and closes.

Mary Wilson-Formerly-of-The-Supremes

Her warm-up is elephants: "A" and "B"
read the rhinestone medallions draped between
their wise and human eyes. Everyone loves
an animal act. Corseted, sequined,

she dances out of the slide-step decade
she spent behind the Queen of R & B
whose part she says she will do. Backing her,
a boy whose gender means he can't compete
and a hip-heavy braless ingenue
who worships her. At halftime when she calls

for volunteers, for someone who always
wanted to be a Supreme, Michael T.,
a hairdresser from Minneapolis
who's come alone, smooths his flamingo shirt
and squares his shoulders to adjust his lime
green satin sport coat. He takes the stage. *Stop!*

in the name of love, he sings, his right hand
palming the audience. Oh he knows all
the words by heart. He knows all the right moves.
In short, he steals the show.

My Mother's Eye

In life, my mother's eye
is small, lashless,
a bead drawn on my back
since childhood. Nothing
escaped her. Now
through the cataract's conspiring cloud,
she sees two of me, doubly wrong.

Eye of amber, cat's-eye, sharp-eyed
owl, homeless floater big as a fist
on the monitor in the cubicle
where I sit transfixed, my eyes
on her eye clamped open
as in death's bald, unblinking
stare, I navigate the three rings
of the planet Eye, its fissures, folds
of secrecy—what she keeps
even from herself: years of great
depression, stupefying blame,
sorrow's spinning finger
that stops at suicide.

I shrink from the usual instruments
of clarity—the needle, for instance,
blood let like Ophelia's tendrils loosed
in the fatal stream. The dogs
of the past are swimming for their lives.
One by one they are hooked and collared,
dragged offscreen grinding terror
between their teeth.

When the new lens wheels across the empty cavern
of my mother's eye, flanges unfurling,
memory's black hole fills
with anemone, blossom, and star.

A Matter of Interest

Blank sky, blank check,
memory's swamp is sunk.
Traveling the Illinois prairie,
my daughter beside me
lists what to look forward to.
She wishes on every white horse.
Her vocabulary quiz
consists of fifteen words beginning
with the letter *A: anticipation,
acumen, alacrity.* She's learning to drive.
I'm anxious. But marking the distance
between one farm and the next,
what accrues is space.

II

Guilt I

It's not the torment Hieronymous set down
Nor the retractable fruit Tantalus cursed.
The land of guilt is temperate, palm and frond,
Where every apple ripens, fleshed to fit your hand.

Guilt II

In the usual story of loss, a traveler sets out on foot
with all he owns on his back. Never mind his dili-
gence, everything's taken by force or tomfoolery. His
step grows lighter even as his sorrow deepens. Soon
he begins to sing. The other travelers, envying his
song, hunger after him, cramming his pack with
the weight of everyone who claims to have been
wronged—the long-suffering wife, petulant child,
the shenanigans of the whole foot-stomping past.
As for him, he accepts every ounce, every grain—
load enough to break a burro, crush stone, seal the
earth's ravenous craters.

The Misery Twins

Blessed are those who know that suffering is not
a crown of glory.
                    —Jorge Luis Borges

1

Bumper butts bumper four lanes across:
we're in a squeeze
on Lake Shore Drive where nothing moves
except the clock,
creeping up on midnight
in this massive metal shut-down,
this gear-grinding crunch,
this needle-tipped-toward-the-red-zone night
that digs in its fingers
like its sister, heat—the misery twins,
scourge of us all
except those touched by rage.
Those they take up in their arms.

Summer's burst on the scene
off cue, cocksure,
mocked by the halogen overhead,
veiled with fumes, smoke,
breathy exhalations of exhaust
spiked by radios' divergent beats—
bass whunking like stones—
wolf whistles, catcalls, aggression's
sad menagerie.
                    Down the stalled rows,
a bangled wrist through a moonroof,
foot through a window, limp as a neck.
Speeding in the narrow aisles,
five toughs on Harleys,
unhelmeted, heedless,

21

yank up their handlebars
to coast on heat, coast on night,
coast on through
as if there were another side.

2

In my new car, the gauges
hold steady. We lounge
in leather, take in
the air-conditioned air.
When we talk, each word
translates into an accident
of our own making.
You berate my weakness,
my hesitation in all things.
To teach me a lesson,
you slap yourself, the hard
staccatos of our undoing.

3

Once, in true summer,
we drove north toward Sorrento
through miles of carbon monoxide–rich tunnels
cut through rock, hardly an escape
from the smoke-choked road
rife with burn-off from the summer fields.
I told you the story of a woman
who burst into flames, a story
lost under the shadow of your disbelief.

In the last long tunnel,
parked cars lining both sides of the road,
you remarked how they rocked on their struts.
Cardboard fitted over their windows
shut each man, each woman,
into the thick dark soup of sex

you invited me to imagine.
But what I saw was this: their eyes
red and burning,
even though huge fans grinding overhead
pushed the poison toward the exit.

So Long

Whitman loved to say it—
those two common syllables
rude on the tongue:
long *o* adrift in his beard,
soft *g* hardly a hook. *So long.*

Kin to every cadence,
it accommodates the iamb's ascending pitch,
the spondee of a door slamming back on itself,
the simple pyrrhics of a childhood sea
unlike the ceaseless sighs that could have struck
Arnold dumb. I have known such sighing:

> *It has been too long,*

although we were afraid to say it—
the easy rhythm that means goodbye.
It was as if martyrdom's needle
had sewn shut our lips.

Seeing you in a dream
after a long absence,
your beard grown long,
down past the ordinary scruff
I always hated, hair
lunging past your shoulders—
Christ, I say, *you look like Whitman.*
So. . . you reply. . . long.

Tennis for Beginners

Our group of four lines up
for a drill: *forehand, backhand,*
forehand, backhand, the teacher instructs
at each toss. Always polite,
we try to hit the ball, not
our teacher, each other, or ourselves.
We know it belongs inside the white lines
marking out tyranny's blocks and boxes,
the little yellow ball that bounces
as if to guide us through the lyrics
of a song we have not yet learned.

When we try our luck
at doubles, I draw Sonny
who wears an artificial leg, steel shank
disappearing into a foam thigh patterned
with the globe's blues, greens, yellows,
and pinks, a restless sweep
of oceans and continents. His real leg's
still in Vietnam, caught in the machinery

of war. Our opponents
come from India, husband and wife.
Arms open, faces lit with hope,
they spoon their balls into the upper air,
gonging the ducts, pinging the wire cages
protecting the lights. With every move
her sari shifts the seasons:
vines of stars circle the palaces of change.

Metal ball swiveling in its metal socket,
Sonny's ready. Unshouldering his racquet,
his false foot charges the net.
When it's my turn to serve, I double-fault.
Visualize, Paulette! Sonny insists.
My next ball flies into the rafter's odd geometry

where it sticks. Since we are unschooled
in the protocol of who stands where
in this game where *love* means *nothing,*
our teacher keeps score. *Deuce!*
he calls. Sonny shouts my name.
Glancing upcourt, I see him red-faced, raging,
his body fleshed with its true weight.

Chinese Acrobat, Age Six

Beijing, 1995

He's supple as the swan's long neck,
spineless as a wandering eye.
Such cunning at elbow and knee!—
strangers to angularity:
first he's a snake biting its own tail,
then folded in half, he fits in a jar:
tipped on its side, he wriggles out,
his lipsticked lips gymnastic,
this Child of the Perpetual Smile
trained to please by the woman
who stands behind him with a stick.
For every inch he fails to grow,
she rewards him. Nightly,
he inspects himself at every hem,
but history's written
on his skull's intractable plate:
inside the boy resides the future man.
When he bows, his back
twisted into punctuation
for the question he will one day ask,
the audience applauds
as if this were another stunt.

Frozen Shoulder

How unlikely the doctor should call it
the *center of coldness,* the shoulder,

always malingering on the sidelines,
the shoulder, and not

the mind, deep in the skull's dark crypt,
stuttering in its icy rut,

or the heart, little pendulum,
agoraphobic as ever,

not the heart, but its homely neighbor,
the left shoulder, hunched like a judge

over the left hand, purveyor of secrecy,
yes, the shoulder, that master

of exclusion leading the back
as it turns away from invitation,

turns away from the husband, the mother,
the sister, turns again

out of habit, perversity, inattention,
and after decades of such turning,

after years of travel,
the tired metaphor *cold shoulder*

blunders through the labyrinth of sinew and nerve
to arrive at the frozen wall of refusal

where it butts against bone
then finally hardens into fact.

Hibakusha

The title literally translates from the Japanese as "I met with the A-bomb" or "explosion-affected person." "And survived" remains implicit because the culture considered survival to be disrespectful to those who died.

She has told this story
before, and now she will tell it
again, this story that has been her life
since August 6, 1945, date
burned into her right arm, right thigh,
into every strand of the fallen wing of her black hair,
the frightened animals of her eyes.

After the first word
the others follow, obedient
as dogs on the scent, word after
word with the sound of something small
moving through dry grass.

Pika for the beautiful flash of light, don for the thunder. I was twelve, a schoolgirl in uniform when the siren said all clear, but when I woke for the second time that day, the bright shining morning was turned to night. All around me, the blazing willows, the blazing cherry trees.

My clothes are burnt off. My friend is disappeared, my classmates—disappeared. I am hot. I need to drink water, I need water to cool my body. I am burnt, my face and hands are burnt, my arm, my leg, whatever part of me was not flat on the ground, burnt. I think only of the river. A girl I know pleads to me with her eyes to take her with me, but I cannot help her. I feel ashamed my hurt is less than hers.

*I vomit, my gums bleed, all my hair falls out. "I
should be burnt instead," my mother says, "I am so
old and easy to die." For nearly a year she will not
let me look. When I finally find myself in the mirror,
I see a monkey.*

*In Osaka, I become friend to the knife to make my
eyes open and close, my fingers uncurl, to take the
cancer from my stomach. Later I cross an ocean for
a face a man can bear. But how can they know what
kind of baby? So, I still living alone.*

*I do not want to blame, I do not want apology. I
come only to tell my story, nothing more. Thank you
so much, thank you so very very much.*

Guest in this world, *hibakusha,*
leper no man will touch,
you unbutton your right cuff
and let fall the sleeve
that bunches at your elbow like skin.
Here is an arm that means
the next seat is always empty,
here is the long arm of the past slick as an eel
that won't swim away
but lingers in the shallows of your body.

Witness, we are your witnesses
come to take this story
as the current takes the lanterns
floated each August down the Ota,
its surface reminiscent with flame;
as the wind takes the paper cranes
heaped beside the bombed dome
whose unfleshed ribs
still incite the sky, meaning
we shall not repeat the evil,
we shall not repeat the evil.

Summons

On my birthday

In my left ear pressed against the pillow in dawn's
half light, I hear a bell,
one clear tone—
simple as *The museum is closing,*
Fasten your seatbelt, or *Going down*—
but understand the sound's inside
my head, an embryo curled
in the cochlea's dark coil. Like the sea
echoing within the nautilus
that articulates its vacancies
only to you who hold
its chambered beauty ear against ear.

I know a man who reads simultaneously
five different translations of *The Duino Elegies,*
one for each sense to apprehend. But
I speak of one note, beautiful and insistent:
this has only to do with you.
Not with your husband breathing above you,
not with the child who once lived inside your body—
even they cannot hear this pure sound.

Call it a summons, a legacy—Adam and Eve
taking that wrong turn, call it the others
dropping away and you shut of everything,
your bones visible through the thin curtain
that has always arrested the eye.
Of course you are alone
in your certainty that I
will step forward, I
who have been hiding behind you,
plotting to send you in my stead.

My Father's Heart on Film

Shot through with dye,
every tributary announces its failings.
Anemones caught in a sudden current
know such motion and the restive fish
unschooled in the larger scheme.
I had thought they knew their place,
like children taught to deserve
the good family name.

When the doctor explains
disease has nursed the heart,
doubled, redoubled
beyond the dimensions of this screen,
I am the true daughter
whose own heart tugs at its root.

Blood thrums in my head,
the sound absent from the silent film
where no timely chord
measures the projector's low hum
or the doctor's seamless murmuring:
here here here here.

When he lifts his finger
to stop the machine, I frame
a wish that the film
become an endless loop,
sympathetic to the real heart
drugged calm in its deep cave,
an island grotto
where blind fish swim unharmed.

Hope

It was lost,
that glittering part of yourself
you wore but not on your sleeve.

OK, turned out
in leafless autumn, a dangerous time,
knee-deep in detritus.

Skulking in a corner
it did not choose—what
sly crevice, niche, or den,

what distant port or coffin,
it accuses you:
graverobber! heretic!,

when you pry it loose:
chink-chink-chink-chink
across the moonstruck macadam.

Catching it up,
its familiar light
decants into your palm.

You call it luck.
Not knowing what's held back,
you try to pocket it.

Anvil, Clock, and Last

My father liked to paint things gold:
the antique clock, its swinging pendulum,
a last designed for an Italian foot,
the blunt-nosed anvil, birthday gift to me.

His picture frames compete with gilded streams,
dazzling lanterns rival paler flames,
and cowbells' muted clappers free their wards.
There's nothing gilt can't solve.

(Once I saved my father's life—
with one quick press unstuck the bone
that threatened breath. No one said a word.
We sat back down. Potatoes, beans, and fish.)

His passion was for plurals:
seven sewing machines, thirteen violins,
twenty hardwood chairs, sentries
at the basement steps, doors to his domain.

His interests rose in increments,
things he'd found on curbs
or trades he'd made to make things his
then overhauled—oiled, glued, and braced,

or stripped and stained, varnished slick as talk:
four accordions, keys to any door,
ninety rifles, air horns, telephones in Bakelite, oak—
bullwhips, barrels, bootjacks, crocks,

fifteen potbelly stoves, zithers, rockers,
wicker trunks from Germany.
He's unstrung five pianos, numbered keys
as neat as headstones on the basement floor.

Collapsed across the sander's double belts
(he never dealt in glass), I found my father
blue, cold. The medics came.
It stopped my breath. Needle, shock, and pill.

Now my father's quit his brushes,
scrapers, spangled paint, he argues
with the clock, its swinging pendulum,
the anvil he can't lift (he gave it once to me).

He's left his mark on everything
time filtered through his hands. He's left
it all to me, his eldest daughter,
the next in line: anvil, clock, and last.

Half of the Story

The car in front of mine has lost control.
It swerves right off the road. Then back again.
It's not the end, but half the story's told.

The driver twists the wheel, sideswipes a pole.
The door caves in like soldiers cast from tin.
The car in front of mine has lost control.

What happened here and who are we to know?
A heart attack, a dream, or failed attention?
It's not the end, but half the story's told.

I floor the brake, resisting calls to follow.
Temptation lures me past the yellow line.
A wilder truth is now I've lost control

but only for the moment that I hold
the slippery dream of giving in.
It's not the end, but half the story's told.

I pass the wreck, let the impulse go.
The driver's face? Anonymous as mine.
The car in front of mine has lost control.
The end? But only half the story's told.

Lucky Death

My father's chair turned toward the picture window
invites me to sit where he sat at daybreak
when his heart stopped.
I look where he looked: down
at the little black dogs, foolish poodles
who followed him for handouts
but stayed after his arms and legs had grown cold—
one on his knees, the other curled at his feet—
stayed after the medics took him away,
and still they stay, stationed on his bed
or at the window, waiting to report all comings
and goings, these two amigos, little sidekicks.

Shelved in mahogany on the wall behind his bed,
ivory horses, Chinese, hold their classic poses:
long necks stretched, arched, or folded muzzle to hoof,
unlike the piebald my father would choose
if he were a redskin or the palomino
that would put him on the side of the law
in the TV westerns he watched morning to night—
the Cisco Kid riding with Pancho, Wild Bill, and Hopalong,
Gene Autry packing his guitar, daredevil Ken Maynard,
the Lone Ranger, that masked man of the plains,
and Tonto—morning to night cowboys and Indians
galloping in black and white, galloping always
left to right as if they were reading the range:
foothills sere and stretching to the Sierran wall,
tumbleweed bumping the saguaro, its arms thrown up
in surrender, galloping past Lone Pine, the last outpost,
galloping deeper into California's Alabama Hills,
dodging between tall spiky rocks and basalt outcrops,
stopping only to sing to the stars.

My father's last task is saddling the horse
named Lucky, a mustang he saved
who knows Diablo, Fritz, and Topper, Champion,

Tarzan the white wonder, and Hi-Yo-Silver-Awa-a-ay!,
horses who could count, add,
dance, or play dead, horses who could warn
their masters of the journey's perils,
who know the way to the ancient pine
twisted by fire and ice
where they'll meet up with my father
who's coming, white hat, white suit,
six-shooter strapped to his hip,
left foot deep in the stirrup,
reins fisted against the horn,
right leg already thrown up and over,
the little black dogs running along behind.

Planting

After three hard freezes,
the experts say, the ground
will be ready to receive
them: crocus, tulip,
hyacinth—bulbs
sullen as potatoes.
Even their names
weigh on your tongue.
All winter they mull
their showy ascension.

Your stiff fingers
and swollen knees
finally forgotten,
your house transformed,
you believe each flower
a gift you don't deserve,
like found knowledge,
or a good daughter
bearing your name into the future.

White Birch

It has known rain in every season,
stored it like knowledge in every cell,
the white birch I used to watch from the window
of my father's house.
How easily it bent beneath the weather
for that is the case with beauty. My father
cut it down himself, sawing the trunk
into logs, not to burn
but to brighten the summer fireplaces
of everyone he knew, saving the best for me,
his favorite daughter.

On this winter afternoon of record cold,
I build a fire, rough-cut hardwood,
stored in the garage for years, dry as old leaves.
Its burning punctuates the separate stories
we read. When you add more logs
I don't look up, although I'm glad for help.
Later, at your urging, I put down my book to admire
the fire's even burn. There among the cradling flames
like the walking Meshack between friends,
three logs, not split like the others
but whole, round, recognizable.

I try to explain how, each spring, I puzzled together
those suedey limbs, the ceremony of finding the perfect fit,
and how it brought back a childhood of arranging—
books on the shelf, tiny plaster figures around the creche,
all the idle hours. Year after year,
the birch under my hands
fell to the same configuration, like the living tree
that remembers how much give resides in its branches.
Once, in a dream,
my fingers marked with its fine white powder,
I heard the words *Skin, not bark* so clearly
they woke me.

But how can I call this loss
when others have felt a young hand
slip from theirs forever
or see a funeral in every fern?
And is it loss, after all, when the last embers
have died on the grate,
if in memory my father's birch still blazes?

After the Funeral

My dream confirms it:
heaven is up,
earth's below.
Housed on his island of clouds,
my father—buried today.

Dropped from above,
a thick two-handed rope.
I have climbed a long way
to enter this picture.
My arms ache.

Reaching over the edge,
he pulls me up.

IV

Drift

Slow creep of juniper over its island of rock,
the cat in her self-made prison i.e. any moving square of light,
a spirea's white arms waving goodbye to winter as season drifts
    into season almost beyond notice but no less true: *Suddenly,*
    you say, *the world's green—*

summer crowds pressing toward a higher note,
a castrato's young voice rising like incense into the vaults of glory,
    which brings to mind

fire in its infancy climbing the hill's brown slope,
the errant petal of your tongue against my lip.

All my life I have loitered under the indolent shadow
of the past. Unloosed, the dark drift
of my hair crosses the pillow's white ocean to find you.

*There is a beach where I have lain, where waves adored me head
to foot, turned me on my back, packed my suit with sand, cup to
crotch.*

Or was that a dream?

Adrift in a different year: behind me
the white cliffs of Dover dull, dim, and fade.

The hand closes, the hand opens.

Live ash flicked from a night car skitters across the asphalt—little
comet, little fantail, bright filament, lit tendril, neon passage. *I
have tracked the stinging threads of the jellyfish awash in the Pa-
cific's uneasy trough, and later the captives, their rare umbrellas
unfurling, their intricate parachutes praising the aquarium's still
waters.*

Was it then that the future,
a woman in a white dress who has always known
which foot to put first,
took up my two hands as if I were blind?

Cold Snap

A man I know is out in it, bent
on a senseless errand. He chafes his hands,
mutters into his frozen beard. If
he returns, he will tell stories
of pigeons fallen like stones
from their perch under the El
while wondering whether I would mourn
his passing.

In the news, a woman's frozen to her floor
in the usual attitude of prayer. Taking her
for dead, the medics joke over a joint
while they chip at the ice. Consider
their surprise when she mumbles an invocation
to whatever saint knows firsthand
cold that cuts to the bone.
When he appears, she holds out a hand
she expects to be taken.
The medics, who think she is waving, wave back,
although she has already boarded a ferry
to nowhere they can imagine.

Hearing this, I wish for his return, sorry
for my small cruelties, willing,
after all, to run out across the frozen ruts,
my breath draping the air like a white flag of surrender,
bitter air biting the soft, pink, uninitiated
tissue of my lungs, run until I trip. One knee
addresses the unyielding ground.

In this version, it's night—a starless field.
Still kneeling, I wait for him to appear,
take me up and hold me close enough
to hear my heart longing to escape its own longing,

choosing to believe
I have found the excuse I needed
to kneel before him
who long knelt before me.

The Woman Always Turns First

Although he is dancing with himself,
our teacher says it again: *The woman always
turns first.* Circling the ballroom,
his bare feet long and thin as blades,
soundless gliders I remember from girlhood winters
in the flooded park, he twirls
his woman of air. Right pant leg rolled
so we could tell right
from left, see which foot leads
as he shifts from waltz to foxtrot, from cha-cha
to rumba to polka, white leg scissoring
the black one as he quicksteps across the polished floor.
The imaginary woman he holds
is perfect, compliant, and although she knows
she must follow, she listens to him repeat *The woman
always turns first.* Yet

you have turned from me. For the first time
the bones of your back
rebuff me as you turn to the past
where only a woman-you-had-to-imagine
took your hand or climbed with her fingers
the bony ladder of your body or
knelt over you and praised you
with the warm circle of her imagined sex,
thus disproving the proverb we've been taught
by Randy, King of Ballroom Dance, *The woman always
turns first* said more times than we can count,

but finally the hand you take is mine. Innocent
as crumbs, we walk the leafless wood in early spring,
a wildflower path where you identify
the first mute trillium, bloodroot,
wild violets you mistake for bloodroot
and pull up to see if the root is red,
split with your nails to see

if it will bleed because you are certain
the heart leaf is bloodroot and only bloodroot
and you will make it bleed into your hand,
pool in your palm, exceed
the cup of flesh, rive the deep beds of decay
their leaves rife with spores,
and spill into the deep, clean
prints of horses gone before us, hoofprints
cut like biscuits into the swampy ground
that sucks our shoes as if to pull us
down, drown us in the forced blood
of your certainties *the woman always turns
first* we come to a stump,
lichen frilling its length on the east,
tiered and radiant, green fans
like oyster shells, blood tide
rising, lichen wildly
remaking itself, flowering
from the crumbling stump.

The Break of Day

After Paul Delvaux

They are still women,
these sisters, Daphne's kin.
See how they pose their movable arms
but defer to their rooted feet?
They are already
settling into the future,
long white dresses
shed in a heap,
everything coming undone.

Only one is surprised
by dawn's indifferent light:
the one with legs,
in the distance,
who looks back
into the sun's bright mouth.

She does not see
the man in black
begin his morning walk
past the pillars
whose shadows branch like trees,
out among the stones,
whatever they may be.

He walks at leisure
toward the foreground
now in shade,
twists a stubborn limb.
When he lifts his hand again,
the arbor spills its vines
that dip and rise like startled flocks,
a swallow blooming from each bloom,
a garland for the breaking day.

Elephant Seals at Point Piedras Blancas

1

Hand over hand
we scale a fence
to reach the breeding beach
replete with the long gray length of them,
sleek as torpedoes, still as stones.
Hand in hand we walk among them
the Pacific unfurling behind us,
although I alone
kneel at the flukes of a sleeping bull
and stroke with four fingers
the slender edge,
hand given over into my hand,
stroke the much-to-be-desired fur according
to the direction of its growth, stroke
the path the ocean smoothed
through long years of immersion,
stroke the one I chose, this bull at rest,
his fellows massed around him
like the suburbs of a great city.

When he wakes,
I look into his eyes that carry their own brand
of intelligence and find them willing, kind.
I could lie down beside him
to better survey his hide crosshatched with history,
each grain of sand dug
into each crease and whorl,
each drop of blood clotting his torn side
testament to rivalry's flash and nip.
I could take in his bull scent,
his snuffle and huff,
lick his salt skin, lick it like a pup,
even though I have watched him rear back,
balance on the stumpy webs

of his forelegs, flaunt the shocking
excess of his snout
and roar down his adversary.
I have tracked each reverberation
into the radiant pink cave of its origin.

          Turning my back
to him, I smile into your camera
first asking you to warn
me of any sudden move, as if
a warning could save me from this bull
who could outswim me in the ocean,
outrun me on sand,
butt me down with his great chest
and take his whole weight
across the bony washboard
I call my body.
            But I kneel unharmed,
I who have knelt in danger at your knees,
you who have brought your weight down on me
and groaned as though all were lost,
then slept under my hand
as if it could guide you
through sleep's vast continent.

2

          In my dream,
our boat is a hollow tree.
Since it longs for its own kind
we are conveyed through rushing prairie
toward a forest,
me remembering Isaiah—*All flesh is grass,*
you dipping the single oar into sedge.
We travel without pausing for danger
although it surrounds us.

          But when you lay down
the oar, you will find my hand

in both of yours,
and although I am neither cold nor ill,
you will take it up,
stroke it fingertip to wrist,
wrist to fingertip,
stroke it with a sound like grass,
blade against trembling blade
in this blessèd ocean of grasses:
fescue, foxtail, cocksfoot, panic, love.

Too Much

You have given me
too much: two pearls, two moons ascending—
luminous, miraculous,
like your two hands as I see them in dreams.

Consider this:
loving you contradicts every hard lesson
I have learned, as in:
Never take anything too precious to lose.

Yet, I have taken you.
At night, I listen to your heart through the thin wall
of your chest. Listen,
I could take your heart in my hand,

a pearl. Once, a pearl
was taken up in the mouth of my cat but given
back into my hand,
hand you put to your mouth. Because there is not

enough time, last night
I dreamt of you again: how, as in life, you led me
with your two hands
into another world: a garden

where we have walked
in fact, and so I recognize the music of its streams,
the irises mouthing
their private language of flowering,

and the bridge—
the one we crossed, a Japanese bridge,
here in this garden
in moonlight, too beautiful to bear.

Leaf and Wing

Unshared, your joy outgrows you.
You have to wake me:
>seven grosbeaks, a backyard flock you've counted more
than once, present their rose breasts like little Marys
whose two hands hold a heart against her heart. Anyone
would say it's still early, but you've been up for hours.
Like parents we look down on them from the second-
storey bedroom door,
their black backs dull as stones.

Together we scrutinize their vestments, the scalloped edges
descending to a vee where the rose medallion
>dangles on the male breast (nothing's ever black or white),
matching the facts in the *National Audubon Society Field
Guide to North American Birds*. (I've dreamt about the
closed wing opening, the hidden patch of red.)
You think the feeder coaxed them here,
a contraption you contrived with conduit and duct tape,
planted, greased, and baffled against squirrels,
then stocked with black-oil sunflower seeds.

When the day pauses with its arms around us,
>why do I think of the rhododendron you planted by the
garbage can, flats of English ivy, tight-fisted marigolds,
the clump of purple iris you dug up in Indiana to edify
the rock?
Every window box, trellis, and bed you touched
taught me trust.
The hostas send out their long-stemmed blossoms.

Unheeded, the clock still ticks its usual warning.
I lean into you standing behind me at the open door
(we haven't moved)
>while a dozen grosbeaks feed on the ground—seeds the
purple finches flung like pennies, or the flurries of black-

capped chickadees, goldfinches, or the hairy woodpecker
that clings to the plastic cylinder as if it were an oak.
Already blessed with all that we can bear,
a sudden swoop of indigo, a bunting
clothed in Mary's color,
Mary clothed in sky.

Up here, we're higher than the redbud tree,
a sapling whose branches
bend beneath the weight of their own beauty,
and while you retabulate the grosbeaks,
two northern orioles, a traveling pair,
shift their bright weight
from branch to branch,
proving beauty irresistible to beauty.

Nietzsche said *No evil man can sing.*
Yesterday you spoke their names: *oriole, indigo:*
today they're here.
I listened to your words,
I who've waited years for you,
you who stand behind me now, leaf and wing,
your hands gracing my shoulders,
you whose name I spoke before I knew you,
name that called you here.

Trust

It's a place to fling yourself into from whatever platform, springboard, raft, or tippy boat into whatever Corpus Christi warm or bone-shocking mountain-fed murky-as-sin wave luminous with whatever, not to mention time, fate, and circumstance—they make no difference. The moment that double-thumps the heart more surely than shoplifting or booking passage on a Russian jet, the poet says, is the drop that may take years in its bright abandon: the predator above the certain back of its prey.

Old enough to know better, once I threw heels over head in a reckless flip I hadn't tried since high school. Glad to be alive, I swam up out of that churning world to stand in line again. Turn after turn, feet first or in the off-just-a-little backslapping sting of the surface-become-wreckage, I kept each lung-bursting strap-breaking slip-through-your-fingers date with vertigo I had come to expect.

Remember the game called Trust? Girls falling like dominoes, some with crossed fingers, others crossing themselves before dropping back into indifferent space or the net of hands for which they hoped.

NOTES

EPIGRAPHS

Elizabeth Bishop's lines are from "The Shampoo" in *A Cold Spring*.

Vicente Aleixandre's lines are from "The Explosion" in *Twenty Poems,* translated from the Spanish by Lewis Hyde and Robert Bly.

SO LONG

Stanza two refers to Matthew Arnold and his melancholic speaker in "Dover Beach."

HIBAKUSHA

This poem is dedicated to Miyoko Matsubara.

Fifty-one years after the bombing of Hiroshima, Miyoko Matsubara told her personal story of the events of August 6, 1945, at the University of Chicago, the site where the first self-sustaining nuclear chain reaction occurred, thus proving the theory. At the time of the explosion, she was a twelve-year-old student at a junior high school located one mile from the epicenter. Of the school's 250 pupils, 50 survived.

In stanza three, *pika-don* is a colloquiallism for the atomic bomb. *Pika* means "flash of light," and *don* suggests the sound of the explosion.

The final stanza describes the skeletal remains of the Hiroshima Industrial Promotion Hall, renamed the A-bomb Dome, which have been left as a reminder of the devastation.

The repeated last line is from the inscription on the cenotaph in Hiroshima's Memorial Peace Park, which reads:

> Let all souls here rest in peace
> For we shall not repeat the evil.

ELEPHANT SEALS AT POINT PIEDRAS BLANCAS

The male elephant seal can grow to a length of twenty-two feet and is sufficiently agile on land to bend its head over its back to attack an enemy at its tail.

TRUST

"The poet" is James Dickey, who, in the following lines from "The Heaven of Animals," describes the heaven of predators:

> They stalk more silently
> And crouch on the limbs of trees,
> And their descent
> Upon the bright backs of their prey
> May take years
> In a sovereign floating of joy.